CW01512854

Original title:

Silent Paths

Author: Eliora Lumiste

ISBN HARDBACK: 978-1-80561-041-0

ISBN PAPERBACK: 978-1-80561-602-3

In the Depths of Quiet Reflection

In the stillness, shadows play,
Thoughts wander like leaves in sway.
Whispers of time gently speak,
Echoes of wisdom, soft and meek.

Stars above twinkle serene,
Lost in the night, a peaceful scene.
Heartbeats linger, moments freeze,
Finding solace in the breeze.

Memories drift on a silver stream,
Carried away like a fleeting dream.
In the depths, my spirit soars,
Together with the world, it explores.

Each breath unfolds a tale untold,
In solitude, a treasure to hold.
Reflections dance in the moon's glow,
Revealing secrets we long to know.

As shadows fade with the dawn's light,
I emerge from the quiet night.
With renewed strength, I embrace the day,
In calm repose, I find my way.

A Dance Beneath the Canopy

In the forest, a rhythm unfolds,
Nature's dance, a story told.
Leaves rustle with a gentle cheer,
As the world whispers soft and clear.

Sunlight filters through the trees,
Painting shadows, stirring a breeze.
Birds chirp in harmonious song,
Guiding souls where they belong.

With each step, the earth resounds,
In the space where joy abounds.
Roots that twist in intricate ways,
Holding secrets of ancient days.

Swaying lightly, the branches bend,
In this moment, all worries end.
A ballet of life, wild and free,
Inviting hearts to dance with glee.

Under the stars, we twirl and spin,
Finding freedom deep within.
The melody of the night calls out,
In this dance, we cast aside doubt.

In the Calm of the Wilderness

In the stillness, shadows creep,
Whispers of the night heartily weep.
Stars above, a shimmering quilt,
Nature's grace, in silence built.

Mossy beds beneath the trees,
Songs of crickets dance on the breeze.
Softly moonlight spills its grace,
Painting dreams in this wild place.

River's murmur, sweet and low,
Guides the heart where peace may flow.
Branches sway, to secrets tell,
In this calm, all is well.

Footsteps fade on winding trails,
Every breath, the spirit hails.
Through the wilderness, I roam,
Finding solace, I am home.

Let the wild wrap me tight,
In the calm of endless night.
With each heartbeat, I find bliss,
In the wilderness, I reminisce.

Footprints in Soft Light

On the path where shadows weave,
Footprints linger, gentle leave.
Sunlight filters through the trees,
Brushing earth with golden ease.

Whispers carried on the wind,
Tales of journeys deep within.
Every step a story told,
Memories in soft light unfold.

In the quiet moments shared,
Nature's tapestry declared.
Pausing here to take a breath,
Life's embrace in whispers left.

Footprints lead to realms unknown,
Through the stillness I have grown.
Guided by the softest glow,
In the light, my spirit flows.

With each stride, a dance divine,
In this space, my soul aligns.
Footprints in the softest light,
Mark the journey, pure delight.

Secrets Beneath the Canopy

Underneath the leafy dome,
Nature whispers, found a home.
Mysteries in shadows play,
Secrets held in green array.

Ferns unfurl like ancient scrolls,
Telling stories of lost souls.
Roots entwine, a hidden thread,
Binding life where few have tread.

Sunlight dances, fleeting grace,
In this haven, time and space.
Each leaf speaks of tales untold,
In the canopy, secrets unfold.

Echoes of the past resound,
In this sacred, hallowed ground.
Beneath the boughs, I hear the call,
In nature's arms, I stand tall.

As I wander, heartbeats blend,
With the wisdom forests send.
In the stillness, I can find,
Secrets rich, for heart and mind.

The Quiet Journey Within

In the stillness of my mind,
A journey starts, so rare to find.
Thoughts like rivers softly flow,
Through the valleys, deep and low.

Waves of calm wash o'er my soul,
In this space, I feel quite whole.
Moments linger, softly spun,
In the quiet, I am one.

Searching for the hidden parts,
Echoes of my tender heart.
As I delve into the night,
Finding strength in soft twilight.

Wisdom whispers, gently bare,
In the silence, feel the air.
Stepping lightly, one by one,
Through this journey, I have won.

In the quiet, truth unfurls,
Mapping paths of inner swirls.
With each breath, I grow and sing,
The quiet holds the full offering.

Shadows Beneath the Canopy

In whispers low, the branches sway,
Where sunlight fades, the shadows play.
A dance of leaves in twilight air,
Secrets linger, hidden, rare.

The forest breathes, a timeless song,
Crafting tales where dreams belong.
Each step a note, each glance a thread,
In this realm, the past is fed.

Beneath the boughs, a world concealed,
Stories waiting to be revealed.
Footfalls soft on ancient ground,
In the silence, lost souls found.

Moonlight drips like silver rain,
Casting spells upon the terrain.
Where creatures stir and silence reigns,
Nature's pulse, the heart that gains.

Time stands still in this embrace,
Every shadow, a fleeting trace.
Underneath the canopy's veil,
Whispers weave a mystic tale.

Unspoken Trails in the Mist

A path unfolds where few have tread,
Veiled in fog, where whispers spread.
Each step a choice, each breath a sigh,
In this realm, the past drifts by.

Leaves like secrets cling to trees,
Telling tales only the wind can seize.
Footprints lost in twilight's haze,
Every turn, a different phase.

Glances shared, but words unspoken,
In the mist, old bonds are broken.
Through the veils of time we roam,
Finding threads that lead us home.

Curves of earth, a gentle guide,
In the soft embrace of night, we bide.
Silent echoes call the brave,
To uncover the lives we crave.

As dawn's first light begins to gleam,
The trails dissolve like fleeting dreams.
In the mist, the heart beats fast,
In unspoken paths, our souls are cast.

The Language of Quiet Roads

Winding paths beneath the trees,
Carry whispers on the breeze.
Each road tells tales of days gone by,
Where memories linger, soft as sighs.

Cobblestones worn by time's embrace,
Each step a journey, each space a grace.
In the stillness, the heart can hear,
The language spoken from far and near.

Overhead, the clouds drift slow,
In their shadows, secrets grow.
Hidden joys in corners tight,
Travelers guided by fading light.

Echoes of laughter, faint but clear,
Remind us of our loved ones near.
On quiet roads, we find our way,
In every moment, night or day.

With every turn, we greet the past,
In this journey, the die is cast.
The roads we wander softly show,
The language that connects us so.

Secrets Beneath the Overgrowth

In tangled vines, the world unfolds,
Hidden stories, silently told.
Beneath the green, life finds a way,
Eternal secrets beneath the sway.

Footsteps hushed on mossy ground,
Ancient whispers all around.
Mysteries wrapped in nature's cloak,
In every rustle, truths invoke.

Ferns unfurl in quiet grace,
Guarding tales in this sacred space.
Over the roots, the shadows stretch,
In stillness, the heart can sketch.

Fragrant blooms, their colors bright,
Veil the secrets held from sight.
As daylight fades to twilight's glow,
The overgrowth hums soft and low.

Every leaf, a witness rare,
To the lives that wandered there.
In the thickets, we search and find,
The delicate threads that bind mankind.

When Silence Sings

In quietude the whispers grow,
A melody the soft winds know.
Echoes of dreams in stillness rise,
Where hopes take flight beneath the skies.

The heartbeats pause, the world remains,
Each breath, a note in gentle strains.
With every moment, time takes wing,
In the space where silence sings.

Flickering shadows dance on air,
The universe cradles every care.
In silence, truths emerge and play,
Unraveling night, embracing day.

Letters of light without a sound,
In hushed tones, life's essence found.
An orchestra of thoughts unfurled,
Serenading the waiting world.

When silence wraps us in its grace,
We find our voice, we find our place.
From the depths, our spirits spring,
United in the songs we bring.

The Uncharted Silence

In twilight's blush, the silence sprawls,
An unmarked road, no need for calls.
Footsteps light, as shadows creep,
In depths of thought, the dreams we keep.

Beyond the noise, a stillness calls,
An echo lost in nature's halls.
We seek the paths that few have tread,
Where whispers linger, lightly spread.

The world unspooled in quiet tones,
A tapestry of untold bones.
With every breath, the moment sways,
In uncharted silence, time decays.

A canvas waits, devoid of sound,
Where unseen wonders can be found.
In every pause, life's secrets gleam,
Embraced within the silent dream.

The uncharted paths draw us near,
A soft invite to shed our fear.
In silent realms, new tales we'll weave,
In the quietude, we dare believe.

Steps in the Hollow Light

In hollow light, the shadows play,
A dance of dusk, a fleeting ray.
With careful steps, we trace the line,
Of dreams that shimmer, pure divine.

Each breath evokes a slumbered past,
A history built, from first to last.
In hollow light, the echoes ring,
Filling the void with hope to bring.

The heart beats strong in fragile night,
With every pulse, the world ignites.
In twilight's glow, we dare to roam,
Finding paths that lead us home.

A whisper here, a shadow there,
In hollow light, we shed our care.
With eyes wide open, and souls that fly,
We make our mark against the sky.

Every step unveils a tale,
In the hollow light, we set our sail.
In journey's end, a new dawn bright,
We walk together, hand in light.

A Walk through Unseen Realms

In whispered grace, we take our stride,
Through unseen realms, where secrets hide.
Each step we take, a world appears,
To fill our hearts and soothe our fears.

The air is thick with dreams of old,
Stories wrapped in shadows bold.
With every breath, the magic stirs,
Inviting us where time concurs.

A gentle pull, a silent guide,
Through hidden paths where wonders bide.
In every moment, galaxies bloom,
A dance of stars within the gloom.

We wander wide, where few have trod,
In realms unseen, we seek the odd.
With open minds, we dare to roam,
In twilight's weave, we find our home.

Each echo calls, drawing us near,
In unseen realms, we shed our fear.
A walk through time, where dreams expand,
Together, we will take our stand.

Whispers in the Fog

In morning's hush, the world awakes,
Soft voices drift through silken mists,
Each secret breath, the silence takes,
Nature's sigh, a gentle twist.

Ghostly shapes in shadows dance,
The air is thick with tales untold,
Mysteries wrapped in a trance,
Wrapped in warmth, yet feels so cold.

Step by step the path unfolds,
With every footfall, a story spins,
Lost in dreams as the fog enfolds,
Where the journey of life begins.

Fleeting moments, soft and shy,
Like echoes fading into dawn,
Whispers linger, low and high,
Carried forth as night is gone.

In the realm where shadows blend,
Truth and fiction intertwine,
Seeking hearts, we follow, mend,
In whispers soft, our souls align.

Echoes of Forgotten Trails

Paths once walked now overgrown,
Memories linger, lost in time,
Footprints fade where seeds were sown,
Echoes whisper in the climb.

Beneath the boughs, the stories sleep,
Every stone a tale could tell,
Secrets buried, safe to keep,
Woven in a silent shell.

Wanderers tread with curious eyes,
Drawing lines on the canvas bare,
Tracing steps as the past complies,
In the rustle of the air.

Each step forward, shadows blend,
With the knowledge that we carry,
On these trails, we seek, we mend,
Lost among the paths we tarry.

In the twilight, truth reveals,
The haunt of time, both soft and stark,
In echoes lives, our heart appeals,
To leave behind an inner mark.

The Stillness Between Steps

In moments paused, the silence grows,
Breath held tight in gentle air,
Between the beats, the heart bestows,
A quiet dance, a whispered prayer.

Time stands still, a fleeting grace,
The world around holds its embrace,
Every glance, a sacred space,
In stillness found, we find our place.

Footfalls quiet, echoes linger,
Yet the pulse of dreams ignite,
In every pause, the heart's sweet singer,
Crafting light from depths of night.

With every gap, we're drawn to see,
The beauty held in soft repose,
In the stillness, we find the key,
To unlock what the silence knows.

Though life's a rush, a fleeting tide,
In stillness, seek the truths that rest,
In every break, seek what is wide,
A journey of the soul's true quest.

Shadows of the Unspoken

In twilight's grasp, the shadows loom,
Words unsaid hang in the air,
Silent truths in a dusky room,
The weight of thoughts we seldom share.

With every glance, a story brews,
Veiled intentions within the night,
In secret glances, hidden clues,
Awaiting dawn to bring to light.

The heart aches with what we disguise,
Unraveled dreams drift in the dark,
Yet in the silence, hope still lies,
A yearning flame, a tender spark.

In every shadow's gentle creep,
Resonates what we cannot voice,
Through whispered winds, the spirits weep,
In silent moments, we rejoice.

For shadows speak in colors bright,
Of love and loss, all dreams embraced,
In unseen depths, we find the light,
In shadows cast, the soul is traced.

Counsel of Quiet Places

In gentle woods where whispers blend,
The soft embrace of silence bends.
Among the trees, the secrets dwell,
Each leaf a tale, each breeze a spell.

Beneath the sky, the mind can soar,
With every step, we seek for more.
In tranquil moments, truth reveals,
The soul finds peace, the heart then heals.

The winding paths, both rough and smooth,
Guide weary hearts, their spirits soothe.
In twilight's glow, the shadows play,
A quiet dance at close of day.

The songs of birds, a sweet refrain,
Call forth the joy, release the pain.
Amongst the blooms and fragrant air,
We grasp the beauty, pause and stare.

So let us wander, hand in hand,
Through echoing hills across the land.
For in these realms, our spirits find,
The light of love, forever kind.

Memories Carved in Stillness

In quiet corners of the mind,
Where echoes of the past unwind,
Each moment etched on silent ground,
In stillness, timeless truth is found.

A whisper here, a shadow there,
Of laughter shared, of tender care.
With every heartbeat, stories weave,
In memories, we find reprieve.

The sunlit days and starlit nights,
Are captured in soft, fading lights.
A tapestry of love and grace,
In stillness, we can find our place.

Though time may shift like shifting sand,
These carved impressions, strong they stand.
They guide us through the storms of change,
In stillness, hearts can rearrange.

So when the world feels loud and vast,
Seek out the stillness, hold it fast.
For in that space, we surely see,
The beauty of our history.

The Heartbeat of Abandoned Trails

Where nature breathes, old paths emerge,
Whispers of time in every surge.
With each soft footfall on the ground,
The heartbeat of the wild is found.

Beneath the brush, the stories hide,
Of those who walked these trails with pride.
The echoes linger in the trees,
In every rustle, a secret breeze.

The wildflowers bloom, their colors bright,
A testament to nature's might.
Where silence reigns, we find our way,
In the beauty of an untamed day.

Through tangled vines and over stone,
These ancient ways remind us home.
Each bend a lesson, each rise a chance,
The heartbeat calls us to advance.

So tread with care, embrace the sound,
Of life that thrums beneath the ground.
For in these trails, both old and new,
We find our hearts, forever true.

Tread Lightly, Speak Softly

In gentle whispers, truth takes flight,
With every step, tread soft and light.
The world needs kindness, calm embrace,
In every corner, there's a space.

With words like petals, let them fall,
A sweet reminder, we are all
Connected in this dance of life,
Where love prevails, dispelling strife.

Each voice a note in nature's hymn,
A soft refrain when times are grim.
In every heartbeat, hear the call,
To lift each other, stand for all.

For subtle gestures make their mark,
A glance, a smile, igniting sparks.
To tread lightly on this earth we share,
To nurture hope with tender care.

So let us walk and speak with grace,
In every moment, find our place.
For kindness blooms where hearts align,
Together, in this life so divine.

Gentle Currents of the Unknown

Whispers dance on breezes light,
Silent paths beckon with delight.
Secrets flow like rivers wide,
In shadows deep, where dreams abide.

Stars align in cosmic grace,
Guiding hearts through time and space.
With every turn, a mystery calls,
As night enfolds, and darkness falls.

Softly glimmers hope anew,
In every step, a world to view.
Nature's hands cradle the lost,
In gentle currents, we find our cost.

Beneath the moon's soft silver gleam,
We navigate through every dream.
Embrace the night, for here we roam,
In the unknown, we make our home.

Reflections in the Quietude

Still waters hold the evening light,
Mirroring stars that grace the night.
In tranquil depths, the heart can see,
The whispers of our mystery.

Silence weaves a tapestry,
Of thoughts and dreams, a reverie.
Within the calm, the soul takes flight,
Finding peace in the waning light.

Gentle ripples tell the tale,
Of every joy and every frail.
In quietude, we learn to breathe,
In moments still, we dare believe.

Listen close to nature's song,
In soft embrace, we all belong.
Reflections guide us, hold our hand,
As we create, a life so grand.

Wandering Through the Unseen

Footfalls echo on hidden trails,
Guided by the wind's sweet tales.
Each step reveals the paths unknown,
In quiet realms, we find our own.

Veils of mist shroud the road ahead,
Hints of magic, softly spread.
Where shadows linger, secrets weave,
In wandering, we learn to believe.

Nature's wonders wait in guise,
Beneath the sky's great, watchful eyes.
A journey calls where few have been,
In the depths of the unseen.

With open hearts, we seek the light,
In every turn, a new respite.
Wandering souls, forever free,
In the unseen, our destiny.

The Serene Abode of Shadows

In quiet corners, shadows play,
Where daylight fades, and dreams hold sway.
A gentle hush blankets the night,
In the serene, we find our light.

Silhouettes dance on walls so bare,
Stories linger in the air.
Whispered secrets of times gone by,
In the shadows, memories lie.

Beneath the stars, our thoughts ignite,
Weaving wishes into the night.
In tranquil spaces, hearts unite,
In the abode of shadows, take flight.

Hold the moment, let it last,
Embrace the future, learn from the past.
For in the dark, we find our way,
In the calmest night, light will play.

A Portrait of the Unheard

In shadows softly cast, they tread,
With whispered dreams that go unsaid.
A world that broils with tales untold,
Their silent cries, like embers cold.

Beneath the weight of heavy skies,
They paint their hopes in muted sighs.
A canvas draped in shades of gray,
Where echoes wane and drift away.

Glimmers of light through cracks appear,
Each flicker fueled by ancient fear.
The voices lost within the throng,
A symphony of silent song.

Yet in their hearts a fire burns,
A quiet strength, the world reverses.
In every glance, a story sketched,
Each moment lived, a life etched.

To speak in whispers, strong yet meek,
They find the strength in what's unique.
The unheard trails of ancient art,
A vivid pulse within the heart.

in the Embrace of the Undergrowth

Soft tendrils twist and intertwine,
In dappled light, the secrets shine.
The forest breathes, a gentle sigh,
Where shadows dance and sparrows fly.

Among the roots, the whispers stir,
In every leaf, a hidden blur.
Serenading all who wander near,
In tangled paths, the truth is clear.

Beneath the boughs, the world unfolds,
With stories rich, and dreams of gold.
Each step a journey deep and wide,
In nature's lap, our souls confide.

The mossy beds of ages past,
In stillness found, the die is cast.
Each heartbeat syncs with earth's own pulse,
As nature's grace begins to convulse.

With every breath, the wild renews,
In sacred hush, the heart imbues.
A realm where time and thoughts entwine,
In undergrowth, the stars align.

Silence Between the Leaves

In leaves that flutter, truth resides,
A quiet space where thought abides.
The breeze, a soft and tender muse,
In whispers, all the heart can choose.

Beneath the canopy's embrace,
The world retreats, a gentler place.
Each silence holds a world profound,
In stillness, ancient echoes sound.

A pause that breathes between the notes,
In tranquil waves, the spirit floats.
Each rustle tells a tale of light,
In shadows deep, the stars ignite.

Through leafy arches, time will bend,
As nature's hand begins to mend.
To lose one's self in sacred peace,
Where silence reigns and thoughts release.

The wisdom found among the trees,
In quietude, the heart agrees.
To cherish moments, soft yet bold,
As silence weaves its threads of gold.

The Weight of Still Moments

Time softly rests upon the day,
In fleeting hours, we drift away.
Each moment holds, a weight so fine,
A thousand thoughts in stillness shine.

Beneath the hush, our hopes remain,
In every pause, the joy and pain.
We gather threads of what has passed,
In quiet strength, our hearts are cast.

The stillness speaks, a gentle guide,
In whispered truths, where dreams reside.
Each second stretched, like strands of thread,
In every breath, all words unsaid.

To linger long in soft embrace,
And find the beauty in this space.
The weight of hours, we come to know,
In silence deep, the rivers flow.

For in the pause, the world ignites,
With sparks that flicker through the nights.
The weight of now, a sacred grace,
In still moments, we find our place.

The Lullaby of Distant Echoes

In the night where shadows play,
A whisper calls, soft and gray.
Stars above, they wink and sigh,
A tune that floats, a lullaby.

Through valleys deep, the echoes roam,
Carrying dreams, they find their home.
In every note a heart will beat,
Awake the past, where time feels sweet.

Moonlight dances on the stream,
Cradling thoughts like a gentle dream.
With every wave that kisses shore,
The echoes linger, forevermore.

Lost in silence, voices wane,
Yet their melodies still remain.
In the dusk, they softly fade,
Whispers from the magic made.

So close your eyes, let worries cease,
In distant echoes, find your peace.
With every breath, the night will tell,
The lullaby, a soothing spell.

Guiding Stillness

In the hush where twilight glows,
A stillness deep, tranquility flows.
Amidst the trees, a soft embrace,
Guiding hearts to a sacred place.

Whispers dance on gentle air,
Inviting souls to pause and care.
In quietude, the world sighs,
As stars begin to light the skies.

Moments linger, time stands still,
Nature's canvas, a tranquil will.
Each breath we take, a soothing balm,
In guiding stillness, find your calm.

Let worries fade like morning mist,
In silent grace, exist, persist.
Where echoes meet the softest night,
In guiding stillness, hearts take flight.

So gather close, let silence speak,
In tranquil realms, we find the peak.
With every heartbeat, gentle flow,
Guiding stillness, forever glow.

Nature's Lament in Silence

In the woods where silence reigns,
Leaves whisper low, bearing pains.
A sepulcher of stories lost,
Nature mourns, and echoes frost.

The rivers weep, their waters slow,
Beneath the weight of ages' woe.
Mountains stand in solemn grace,
Guardians of this sacred place.

In twilight's grip, the shadows grow,
Calling forth what we do not know.
Every branch a tale to share,
Loaded with grief, a whispered prayer.

The sky above, a canvas gray,
Threads of sorrow in light's decay.
Yet in this silence, beauty thrives,
A lament where true life survives.

So listen close to nature's song,
In every note, we all belong.
A tapestry of loss and grace,
Nature's lament, our warm embrace.

A Serenade to the Unknown

In shadows deep, the unknown waits,
A serenade that softly fates.
With every step, the heart will sway,
Embracing paths that lead astray.

The moonlit road, a whispered call,
Inviting one and all to fall.
In twilight's hue, the secrets blend,
A journey where beginnings end.

Mysterious winds lift softly sung,
Carrying tales that once were young.
Voices linger in the air,
A serenade, a sweet affair.

Each heart a note, in time's great score,
A symphony of what's in store.
As shadows dance, they intertwine,
In the unknown, our lives align.

So take a breath and leap anew,
In the serenade, find your view.
For in the depths of fear and doubt,
The unknown sings, a timeless route.

Hushed Moments Under the Stars

In the stillness of the night,
Whispers float on gentle air,
Stars blink like secrets shared,
Moonlight paints the world rare.

Crickets sing their soft refrain,
Nature hums a lullaby,
Each heartbeat feels the same,
Beneath the vast, endless sky.

Time stands still in this embrace,
Dreams dance lightly, take their flight,
Within the shadows, I find grace,
In the beauty of the night.

Fleeting moments intertwine,
As echoes of laughter fade,
In this secret, I will dine,
Memories softly invade.

With every twinkle, a wish,
In the silence, peace prevails,
Wrapped in a starlit bliss,
The universe gently exhales.

Traces of the Unheard

In the chill of lonely winds,
Silent voices call my name,
Echoes of where life begins,
Fleeting moments, yet the same.

Footsteps linger on the roads,
Whispers lost within the trees,
Stories carried, heavy loads,
Written softly on the breeze.

Unseen shadows paint the ground,
With secrets tucked beneath the night,
In the stillness, they resound,
Life's tapestry, woven tight.

Faint delights of days gone by,
Memories hidden from our eyes,
Silted dreams beneath the sky,
Where hope and longing softly sigh.

Ghostly echoes linger near,
Tracing paths we used to tread,
In the quiet, they appear,
Words unsaid still glow like red.

Solace of Overgrown Memories

In gardens where the wild things grow,
Whispers of the past are found,
Tangled vines like tales bestow,
Reminders softly wrap around.

Old photographs in fading light,
Captured moments, held so dear,
Time has turned them into flight,
Still, their essence lingers here.

Each petal carries all the dreams,
Of laughter lost, of joy once bold,
In the silence, the heart redeems,
What life concealed, now unfolds.

Rustling leaves tell stories sweet,
Beneath the branches, shadows play,
In memories, time finds its seat,
Waiting for the dawn of day.

Beauty in the overgrown,
In wildness, peace finds its grace,
Ancient roots and seeds once sown,
Together they create a space.

Muse of the Muffled Breeze

A breath of wind through fields so wide,
Carries tales both old and new,
Secrets from the mountainside,
A gentle muse, whispering true.

With each touch upon my skin,
Memories awaken, softly stirred,
The melody of where I've been,
Cradled in the hush of a word.

Veiled visions in the twilight,
As nature folds its fading light,
The breeze composes without fight,
A symphony through endless night.

In the rustle, I find my song,
Notes of solace, pure delight,
A resonating heart so strong,
Guided by the breath of night.

May I wander where you lead,
In the sighs of earth and skies,
Your echoes plant the soul's deep seed,
Awakening the dreamer's guise.

Muffled Echoes of the Heart

In shadows cast by twilight's hue,
Whispers of dreams drift soft and low,
Every sigh a tender cue,
Muffled echoes pulse and flow.

Lost in realms where silence dwells,
The heart converses without a sound,
Tales of love the darkness tells,
In this stillness, truth is found.

Footsteps linger on paths untread,
Each pause a moment etched in time,
Words unspoken, yet widely spread,
Harmony in heartbeats rhyme.

Moonlit glow on tranquil streams,
Reflections dance, elusive light,
Weaving through forgotten dreams,
Muffled echoes in the night.

In the quiet, pain subsides,
Hope springs softly to the fore,
Muffled echoes, love abides,
Within the heart, forevermore.

Solitude Beneath the Branches

Beneath the branches, shadows play,
Whispers of leaves in the breeze,
Nature hums a soothing lay,
Solitude wraps, a gentle tease.

Sunlight filters through the green,
Dancing lights on woven tales,
In this hush, I find the scene,
Peace flows in like gentle gales.

Every rustle, a soft sigh,
Birdsongs drift in sweet retreat,
Underneath the vast blue sky,
Solitude, my heart's heartbeat.

Time stands still among the trees,
Moments stretch like shadows long,
Embraced by nature's soft ease,
In silence, I feel so strong.

With every breath, I am alive,
Nurtured by the earth and sky,
In solitude, my spirit thrives,
Beneath the branches, I can fly.

Veils of Stillness Unfurled

In the morn where silence dwells,
Veils of mist wrap dreams anew,
Nature speaks in tender spells,
Softly weaving shades of blue.

Gentle ripples kiss the shore,
Quiet moments, hearts at rest,
Whispers linger evermore,
In stillness, we are truly blessed.

Sunlight breaks through, warm and bright,
Time unfurls its quiet grace,
In the hush, we find the light,
Veils of stillness, a warm embrace.

Clouds drift lazily above,
Painting skies with fleeting dreams,
In this calm, I feel the love,
Stillness flows like gentle streams.

As night descends, a deeper peace,
Stars emerge in silent cheer,
Veils of stillness never cease,
In their depths, we hold what's dear.

The Hushed Passage of Time

In the dusk, time softly sighs,
Each moment slips like grains of sand,
Beneath the watchful, starry skies,
The past and present gently stand.

Whispers of hours drift away,
Like autumn leaves in quiet flight,
Memories linger, wild and gray,
In the hush, they seek the light.

Every heartbeat marks a change,
Life flows in rivers, wide and deep,
Paths we take, both sweet and strange,
In silence, these we choose to keep.

Fleeting shadows tell the tale,
Of laughter lost and dreams reclaimed,
In the gentle night, we sail,
Through the echoes, we are named.

The world spins softly, night to day,
Time a partner in the dance,
In every breath, though secrets play,
The hushed passage grants us chance.

The Still Waters of the Mind

In quiet depths, thoughts gently flow,
Reflections dance, soft and slow.
A tranquil world, where ideas bloom,
In the stillness, we find our room.

Whispers of peace, in silence reside,
Calm waters cradle, where dreams abide.
The inner voice sings a soothing song,
In the still waters, we all belong.

Gentle ripples, secrets untold,
Visions unfold, like threads of gold.
Here in the stillness, we start to see,
The depths of our souls, wild and free.

Moments of clarity, bright as the dawn,
Crisp understanding, like the night drawn.
With every breath, the still waters rise,
Reflecting the world under vast skies.

So when storms gather, and chaos reigns,
Return to this haven, escape the chains.
The still waters beckon, serene and kind,
To heal the heart and soothe the mind.

Echoes of Nature's Soliloquy

In the forest, the trees softly sigh,
Their voices raised to the endless sky.
Each whisper tells tales of ages past,
Of life intertwined, forever cast.

Birdsong breaks the morning's embrace,
Melodies drift through time and space.
The rustling leaves, a gentle refrain,
Nature's soliloquy, an artful gain.

Rippled streams play, a shimmering sound,
Life's conversations, in beauty found.
In the meadows, the flowers sway,
Sharing secrets, come what may.

Mountains echo with wisdom profound,
With every heartbeat, we're tightly bound.
The wind carries stories far and wide,
In nature's arms, we boldly bide.

So pause a moment, hear the call,
Nature speaks, inviting us all.
In echoes of wisdom, truth does dwell,
In every note, a sacred spell.

Secrets Shared by the Wind

Softly, the wind whispers through the trees,
Sharing secrets, carried with ease.
A rustle here, a sigh and moan,
Stories of places the wind has flown.

It dances in fields, through petals it weaves,
Telling of loves, and heartbroken leaves.
Each gentle gust holds memories tight,
As shadows and sunlight mingle in flight.

In twilight's embrace, the wind begins,
To share the laughter and sorrow within.
Each breath a promise, a tale to unfold,
Of brave adventures and hearts bold.

It sings of the mountains, the valleys below,
Carrying dreams on its soft, sweet flow.
In the hush of the night, it beckons near,
A symphony played, in silence we hear.

So listen close, to the wind's sweet lore,
For it gathers our hopes, and offers much more.
In secrets shared, hearts can be mended,
Through whispers of wind, our lives are blended.

The Sound of Soft Shadows

As twilight falls, the shadows grow,
Whispering secrets only few know.
In quiet corners, where dreams take flight,
The sound of soft shadows greets the night.

They dance with grace, in muted light,
Casting silhouettes, a gentle sight.
With every flicker, a story unfolds,
In the tapestry woven, the heart beholds.

Each shadow speaks of moments past,
Of laughter and tears, forever cast.
Through quiet rooms, they softly roam,
Reminding us where our hearts call home.

In the still of night, their echoes hum,
A lullaby sweet, where we come from.
Embrace the silence, let it descend,
In the sound of soft shadows, we find a friend.

So let your heart listen, let your soul sing,
In the warmth of the shadows, find what they bring.
For in their soft whispers, we truly see,
A life wrapped in shadows, wild and free.

Hiding in Plain Sight

In crowded streets, I linger near,
A shadow, quiet, masked by cheer.
The laughter rings, but none can see,
The hidden soul that longs to be.

I weave through crowds, a ghostly thread,
Unnoticed smiles, a word unsaid.
In every face, a tale concealed,
Yet in my heart, the truth revealed.

The city hums its vibrant tune,
While I remain a fleeting rune.
In every glance, a fleeting spark,
But in the light, I stay in dark.

What is it like to be set free,
From layers thick, to truly see?
I seek to step into the light,
Yet fear holds tight, a silent fight.

In every breath, a wish takes flight,
To bridge the gap, to claim my right.
But here I stand, within the fray,
Hiding still, in plain sight, I stay.

The Gentle Trace of Memories

In quiet rooms where shadows dwell,
Echoes whisper tales to tell.
Each corner holds a fleeting sigh,
The gentle trace of days gone by.

A faded photograph, a smile,
Reminds me of a precious while.
In tender light, the moments gleam,
A distant past, a waking dream.

The soft embrace of autumn leaves,
A fleeting touch that never leaves.
With every breath, a story spins,
In every heart, where love begins.

The laughter lingers in the air,
The weight of loss, a silent wear.
Yet in the stillness, peace can bloom,
The gentle trace of every room.

Through fleeting time, we learn to weave,
The tapestry of what we leave.
In every heartbeat, every sigh,
Resides the love that will not die.

Where the Heart Finds Rest

In quiet woods where whispers play,
My weary heart can find its way.
With branches swaying, softly pressed,
I seek the place where my soul rests.

A hidden glade, a gentle stream,
A tranquil space, a soothing dream.
With sunlight falling, warm and bright,
I close my eyes, embrace the light.

The burdens fade as shadows shift,
In nature's arms, I find my gift.
The stillness wraps me, pure and true,
And in that peace, I am renewed.

Where birdsong dances, breezes play,
A moment's grace, I long to stay.
This sacred ground, a haven blessed,
Here in the woods, my heart finds rest.

The world outside may roar and fight,
But here, I gather strength and light.
In every breath, I feel the zest,
For in these woods, my soul finds rest.

The Symphony of Forgotten Paths

Upon the trail where few have tread,
The whispers of the past are spread.
Each step I take a note of grace,
In nature's song, I find my place.

The rustling leaves, the gentle breeze,
Compose a tune that puts me at ease.
Each winding path, a story sought,
Of dreams and hopes, of battles fought.

With every corner, new views arise,
The light filters through the ancient skies.
In solitude, a harmony thrives,
In every heartbeat, the world survives.

I listen close to the stories shared,
Of every life that once had dared.
The symphony of time unfolds,
In whispers soft, the past beholds.

Each step a dance to memories past,
A fleeting moment, too sweet to last.
Yet in this journey, I find my part,
The symphony lives within my heart.

Whispers of the Wandering Way

In the hush of twilight's glow,
Softly wander, voices low,
Paths unknown, through shadows creep,
Secrets whispered, dreams to keep.

The moonlight dances on the ground,
Echoes call without a sound,
Lost in thought, yet feeling near,
Each step whispers, calm and clear.

Through the trees, a breeze does sigh,
Nature's secrets, passing by,
Winding trails where thoughts may drift,
In the stillness, hearts uplift.

Stars above begin to shine,
Guiding souls, a path divine,
In the night, a gentle sway,
Whispers guide the wandering way.

Every bend holds tales untold,
In the silence, voices bold,
Trust the journey, let it flow,
Whispers guide where dreams will go.

Echoes in the Stillness

In the quiet, stillness reigns,
Softly echoing through the plains,
Moments linger, shadows fade,
Whispers dance in twilight's shade.

Time stands still, a breath, a sigh,
Echoes linger, passing by,
In the silence, wisdom flows,
Secrets known, yet none disclose.

Nature's pulse beats slow and low,
In the calm, the heart will grow,
Each gentle wave, a soothing balm,
In the stillness, find your calm.

Through the woods, soft whispers weave,
Tales of hope for those who believe,
Finding solace in the night,
Echoes guide with gentle light.

Moments shared in twilight's glow,
In the heart, the echoes flow,
Feel the stillness wrap you tight,
In the shadows, find your light.

The Journey of Hidden Steps

Winding paths beneath the trees,
Whispers carried by the breeze,
Every step, a story grows,
Hidden journeys, only known.

Footprints vanish, time moves on,
In the depths, our hearts respond,
Echoes soft in nature's hall,
Steps unseen, yet felt by all.

In each corner, magic waits,
Life unfolds, as fate creates,
Hidden trails where dreams may roam,
Journey forth, we find our home.

From a distance, laughter plays,
Through the woods, the spirit sways,
Every turn, a chance to see,
The hidden steps that set us free.

Bridges crossed, and rivers wide,
Through the journey, hearts abide,
In the dance of steps we take,
The hidden paths, our souls awake.

Footprints of Tranquility

Upon the shore where waters kiss,
Footprints mark a path of bliss,
Each small step, a tale to tell,
In tranquility, all is well.

Morning light, the sky ablaze,
Footprints guide through gentle haze,
In the stillness, hearts connect,
Every moment, pure respect.

Drifting clouds remove the weight,
Softly whispering, set your fate,
Footprints lead where peace resides,
In the calm, the spirit hides.

With each step, the world unfolds,
Footprints tell of stories bold,
Nature's beauty, here revealed,
In tranquility, hearts are healed.

As the sun dips low and fades,
Footprints linger 'neath the shades,
In the silence, find your grace,
Footprints of peace in time and space.

Dreams on Unmarked Trails

Beneath the stars, our spirits roam,
In search of lands we call our own.
With every step, the wild calls clear,
Whispers of hopes that draw us near.

Through tangled woods, where shadows play,
The path is lost, yet finds its way.
With hearts ablaze and eyes aglow,
We chase the dreams the night will sow.

Each brush of breeze, a gentle guide,
In secret places, we confide.
The moon will light our way tonight,
As we embrace the fleeting flight.

The road unfolds, both wild and free,
In every curve, a mystery.
For in the silence, truth reveals,
The strength that only wonder feels.

So take my hand, let's wander wide,
On unmarked trails, our souls will ride.
In dreams we'll forge a bond so true,
As stars conspire to see us through.

Reflections of an Untamed Heart

In stormy skies, my spirit sings,
A tempest fierce that fiercely clings.
With every beat, my heart's refrain,
An echo of both joy and pain.

Through reckless paths where wild things roam,
I find a place that feels like home.
With every scar, a tale to tell,
Of battles fought in shadows' swell.

The sun breaks through the clouds above,
Beneath it lies my endless love.
For in the chaos, I am free,
An untamed soul, just let me be.

With every pulse, the shadows dance,
In wild abandon, lost in trance.
From highest peaks to valleys deep,
These reflections are mine to keep.

So raise a glass to hearts awry,
To soaring dreams that reach the sky.
For in the wild, I learn to grow,
As nature's whispers softly flow.

Beneath the Veil of Twilight

In twilight's hush, the world unwinds,
As day retreats, the night unwinds.
A tapestry of dreams takes flight,
Bathed in the glow of soft starlight.

The whispers breathe of tales untold,
Where secrets linger, bold yet cold.
Within the twilight's sacred arms,
We find our peace, away from qualms.

As shadows stretch and merge as one,
We dance beneath a fading sun.
With every flicker, doubts take wing,
In twilight's grasp, new hopes we bring.

The colors swirl, both dim and bright,
In that embrace of day and night.
Here lies the promise of what's near,
A world reborn, both calm and clear.

So let us linger, hearts entwined,
In twilight's glow, the stars aligned.
For in this moment, time stands still,
Beneath the veil, our spirits thrill.

Pathways of Quietude

In silence deep, where whispers dwell,
The pathways call, a soothing spell.
With gentle steps, we find our way,
Through tranquil woods, where stillness plays.

The rustling leaves, a soft embrace,
In nature's arms, we find our place.
With every breath, serenity,
A quiet heart, a steadfast plea.

The bubbling brook, a soothing sound,
On winding trails, our souls unbound.
In every corner, peace abides,
As we walk on, with grace as guides.

Beneath the canopies of green,
The world feels more alive, serene.
As sunlight filters through the trees,
We find our truth within the breeze.

So take a moment, linger long,
In quietude, we find our song.
For in stillness, life reveals,
The beauty that the heart conceals.

Horizons of Unspoken Thoughts

In silence, dreams begin to soar,
A canvas vast, with tales in store.
Unspoken words in twilight glow,
Whispers rise where shadows flow.

The heart's desires, a silent plea,
Chasing horizons, wild and free.
Each thought a wave upon the shore,
Breaking gently, seeking more.

Beneath the stars, the mind will roam,
In endless currents, we find home.
With every breath, the world expands,
In unison with hopeful bands.

What lies ahead, a mystery deep,
In quiet nights, our secrets keep.
The moonlight dances on the sea,
A mirror showing what can be.

The Echo of Soft Solitude

In corners dim, a whisper lies,
Amongst the shadows, silence cries.
The echo lingers, soft and low,
A gentle pulse, a tranquil flow.

Lonely trails beneath the trees,
Rustling leaves, the softest breeze.
Each thought a note, a serene song,
In solitude, we grow strong.

The heartbeats dance in measured time,
A symphony of thoughts in rhyme.
Within these moments, peace I find,
A refuge deep within the mind.

As stars emerge, they paint the night,
In solitude, they shine so bright.
A quiet heart knows where to roam,
In whispers soft, we find our home.

Wandering in Reverie

In dreams we drift, where thoughts take flight,
A world of wonder, soft as light.
With every step, the mind explores,
A canvas rich with open doors.

The fragrance sweet of blooming flowers,
In reverie, we sense the hours.
Each moment stretches, time stands still,
As visions swirl, they bend our will.

Through distant lands where colors blend,
We find ourselves, beginnings mend.
In whispers lost, the journey calls,
Our spirits rise, as twilight falls.

The rivers flow with stories past,
In wandering dreams, we breathe at last.
Each thought a brush, a stroke of grace,
In reverie, we find our place.

The Twilight Wisp

At dusk's embrace, the world takes pause,
A gentle sigh, a silent cause.
The twilight wisp, it lingers near,
A fleeting touch, a hint of cheer.

With every hue, the light will fade,
Creating dreams that softly wade.
Through gentle shadows, ghosts will play,
As night devours the light of day.

In whispered tones, stories unfold,
As darkness veils, the heart grows bold.
Each star a promise, shining bright,
Guiding souls through the velvet night.

In twilight's arms, we find our way,
Embracing all that comes what may.
With every breath, the moment slips,
A fleeting wonder, the twilight wisp.

Lost in the Quietude

In shadows deep, I wander slow,
Where whispers soft in breezes flow.
The world outside fades far away,
In tranquil thoughts, I wish to stay.

A gentle hush, the heart's delight,
Amidst the still, the stars ignite.
Each moment blooms, a secret grace,
Time lingers long in this embrace.

The rustle leaves, a songbird's cheer,
Together wrap the soul so near.
In quietude, my worries cease,
With every breath, I find my peace.

Beneath the moon's serene gaze bright,
I shed the burdens of the night.
A calmness swells, a silent vow,
To cherish stillness here and now.

As dawn begins to paint the skies,
I hold the hush, a sweet surprise.
In every pause, I'm slowly found,
Lost in the quiet, fully bound.

Strides of Subtle Discovery

With each small step, the heart unfolds,
New worlds await, in silence told.
The path unknown, yet beckons clear,
Each footfall whispers: persevere.

In every glance, a story grows,
The hidden truths, a gentle prose.
The earth beneath sings softly low,
Inviting me to learn and know.

Through tangled woods and fields of gold,
Adventures hide, treasures untold.
A fleeting shadow, a fleeting sound,
In subtle quests, my joy is found.

The scent of earth, fresh after rain,
Awakens dreams, both wild and plain.
In nature's grace, I find my way,
A dance of life in bright array.

With every pause, a breath to take,
The smallest choice can blaze a wake.
In strides of subtle hope, I roam,
Each moment leads me closer home.

The Unseen Trail Ahead

Through tangled branches, I press on,
An unseen trail, though far from gone.
The thicket thick, the sky turns gray,
Yet in my heart, hope lights the way.

With every branch that bends and sways,
I hear the call of brighter days.
The path unwinds, revealing truth,
A journey born from dreams of youth.

In echoes soft, the whispers play,
The road ahead, a grand display.
Each twist and turn, a chance to grow,
In shadows cast by dreams aglow.

The world extends beyond my sight,
Yet still I walk, in faith and light.
For every step I dare to take,
The unseen trail sends peace awake.

Though fog may hide the end in gloom,
I trust this path will lead to bloom.
In every heartbeat, courage flows,
The unseen trail invites me close.

A Melody in the Air

In twilight's glow, the notes arise,
A melody that softly sighs.
The world joins in a symphony,
Where hearts converge in harmony.

Each sound a wave that sweeps along,
A gentle breeze, a whispered song.
With open ears, the spirit flies,
To dance beneath the starlit skies.

The laughter of the nightingale,
In every note, a wondrous tale.
The rustling leaves add to the score,
A timeless tune forevermore.

As moonlight bathes the earth in dreams,
The melody flows, like glistening streams.
In moments pure, joy takes its flight,
An endless song beneath the night.

With dawn, a hush, yet music stays,
In whispered winds and golden rays.
A melody lives, forever near,
In every heart; it waits to cheer.

Where Shadows Meet the Dawn

In twilight's grasp, the shadows play,
A dance of light, as night gives way.
Whispers of hope in colors bright,
As dawn unveils the tender light.

Silhouettes fade in the morning glow,
With every step, new dreams will flow.
The sky ignites in hues of gold,
A story of the brave and bold.

Each ray a promise, soft and clear,
Chasing away the silent fear.
In the stillness where secrets lie,
The world awakens, hearts soar high.

A journey starts when shadows fall,
In the quiet, we hear the call.
Footprints linger on this warm ground,
Where love and hope can truly be found.

With every dawn, a chance anew,
To chase the dreams we hold so true.
In the embrace of morning's light,
Where shadows meet the hope of night.

The Path of Inner Whispers

In the silence, softly spoke,
The gentle words, like smoke.
Guiding hearts through winding trails,
Where each breath tells hidden tales.

Among the trees, a rustling sigh,
Secrets linger, spirits fly.
In twilight's hush, we pause to hear,
The whispers echo, ever near.

Each step taken, a dance of fate,
In quiet moments, we await.
The song of nature, a tender song,
Reminding us where we belong.

Paths untraveled call us forth,
To venture deep, to seek our worth.
With every whisper, wisdom shared,
Our souls awakened, hearts laid bare.

With eyes wide open, we embrace,
The path of inner grace.
In every shadow, light will find,
The whispered truth within our mind.

Echoes of the Untraveled

Beyond the hills where silence reigns,
A journey starts through endless plains.
Footfalls soft on unmarked ground,
In solitude, new truths are found.

The winds of change sweep through the air,
Carrying dreams, both light and rare.
Each step forward, a tale retold,
Of courage found, of hearts bold.

In valleys deep, where shadows creep,
Echoes of hopes that softly weep.
Yet in the darkness, glimmers shine,
A map unfolds, a path divine.

With every whisper, the past revives,
In echoes bold, our spirit thrives.
Through winding ways, we learn to trust,
In the journey's call, we rise from dust.

The untraveled road, a mystery wide,
Invites the seeker to walk inside.
In every heart, the echoes live,
A promise to learn, a pledge to give.

Reverie Among the Trees

In the forest, dreams reside,
Beneath the branches, side by side.
A tapestry of green and gold,
Stories waiting to be told.

Each rustling leaf, a gentle sigh,
Whispers carried from sky to sky.
In this hush, we find our peace,
A moment where the chaos cease.

Sunlight dances through the boughs,
Time suspends, as here we browse.
In shadows deep, our spirits soar,
As nature's beauty opens doors.

The world outside fades from our mind,
In this reverie, love we find.
Among the trees, we breathe and dream,
Lost in the magic, a shared theme.

With every sigh, a memory grows,
In the silence, our essence flows.
A bond is formed where hearts entwine,
In reverie, our souls align.

Unseen Routes of Solitude

In whispered winds, I walk alone,
Through forest paths, where shadows roam.
I trace the lines of ancient trees,
And find my heart at peace with ease.

The world falls silent, time stands still,
As moonlit streams begin to fill.
I breathe the air, so pure and bright,
In solitude, I find my light.

The hidden trails, like secrets share,
Each step reveals a truth laid bare.
A gentle touch of nature's hand,
Leads me to places rarely spanned.

Through unseen routes, my spirit flies,
A quiet whisper that never dies.
In solitude, my soul will grow,
Unseen routes, where wildflowers glow.

Hidden Corners of the Soul

In quiet nooks, my thoughts unwind,
Where hidden corners, peace entwined.
I seek the depth where shadows play,
And find my solace in the gray.

Among the echoes, dreams are sown,
In every crevice, I feel home.
Soft murmurs speak of love and loss,
A tapestry of gain and cost.

The laughter lingers, joy and pain,
In hidden corners, both remain.
I learn to dance with both my fears,
To celebrate the joy of tears.

Each hidden space, a tale retold,
Of moments cherished, brave and bold.
In shadows deep, I see the light,
Hidden corners, where hopes ignite.

Tranquility in the Thicket

In emerald thickets, calmness reigns,
Where sunlight filters through the grains.
The rustling leaves, a soft refrain,
Whispering secrets, sweet and plain.

Within this grove, I lose my way,
Embraced by nature, night and day.
The gentle hum of life surrounds,
In tranquility, my heart resounds.

A babbling brook, a tranquil song,
Inviting me to stay quite long.
Beneath the boughs, I find my peace,
My restless thoughts at last release.

In tranquil thickets, I unfold,
A tapestry of dreams retold.
Nature's brush paints soft and slow,
In tranquil thickets, my spirit grows.

The Language of Untrodden Ways

In paths unwalked, a voice takes flight,
A language written in the night.
With every step, I dare to dream,
Through unknown trails, I hear the theme.

The whispers speak of what could be,
In silence, I set my spirit free.
Each turn unveils a world anew,
A symphony of dawn's bright hue.

The rustling grass and blooming flowers,
Compose a song through endless hours.
Each leaf a note, each stone a word,
In harmony, my soul is stirred.

The language flows in every breeze,
In untrodden ways, my heart finds ease.
With open arms, I greet the day,
In the language of untrodden ways.

The Lost Routes of Reverie

In shadows deep where dreams reside,
The paths once known shall now confide.
Beneath the whispers of the night,
We wander lost, yet feel the light.

Forgotten trails and secret streams,
Echo the pulse of fading dreams.
In every twist, a story keeps,
The heart's soft yearning, love that leaps.

Among the stars, a gaze so pure,
A fleeting moment to allure.
The memories dance, they softly sway,
Reviving hopes from yesterday.

With every step, we brave the haze,
In twilight's glow, we find our ways.
Through uncharted lands, we'll find our cause,
And write our tale without a pause.

So let us roam this endless maze,
With each turn taken, love's embrace.
In reverie, we're never lost,
For every dream comes at a cost.

Nature's Soft Embrace

With morning light, the world awakes,
In gentle hues, the sunlight breaks.
The dew-kissed grass beneath our feet,
Nature's touch, a rhythmic beat.

The rustling leaves, a whisper soft,
In harmony, the branches loft.
A melody in every breeze,
The songbirds greet among the trees.

Each petal sways, a dance of grace,
In vibrant colors, love's embrace.
The rivers flow, a crystal stream,
Reflecting all our hopes and dreams.

The mountains stand, steadfast and tall,
Guardians of all who hear their call.
In valleys low and skies so wide,
Nature's heart will always bide.

So pause awhile, let tensions cease,
In nature's arms, we find our peace.
Among the wild, our hearts can soar,
Forever touched, forevermore.

A Symphony of the Untold

Beneath the surface, secrets brew,
A symphony that calls to you.
In shadows where the quiet dwell,
The untold stories weave and swell.

In every heartbeat, echoes rise,
A tapestry of whispered sighs.
Each note a tale, both sharp and clear,
Reflecting all that we hold dear.

The silence speaks, a gentle guide,
In every crevice, dreams confide.
A song composed in the still night,
Unfolds like stars, a cosmic light.

From deep within the core of soul,
Emerges music that makes us whole.
With every chord, a life unfolds,
In harmony, the heart beholds.

So listen close, let visions flow,
For in the hush, the truths bestow.
A symphony of all we've known,
In whispers soft, we're never alone.

Where Tranquility Meets the Horizon

Where ocean meets the endless sky,
A tranquil breath, the world goes by.
Sunset spills its golden hue,
A canvas vast where dreams come true.

The waves embrace the shore so kind,
In rhythms soft, our hearts unwind.
Each whisper lures us to the brink,
Where time slows down, and we can think.

In twilight's glow, the night appears,
The stars arise to calm our fears.
Each twinkle speaks of journeys far,
Guiding us softly like a star.

With every sigh from nature's chest,
We find our solace and sweet rest.
In moments still, we chase the dawn,
And greet the day as night is gone.

So let us dwell where gleams the light,
In tranquil spaces, hearts take flight.
For in this peace, we find our home,
Where dreams and souls are free to roam.

Murmured Moments of Clarity

In shadows softly gleaming,
Whispers float on evening air.
Thoughts like leaves in breezes drifting,
Free as dreams that dare to share.

With every breath, a subtle wisdom,
Echoes weave a tapestry bright.
Moments captured in the silence,
Bringing day to dance with night.

Glimmers of hope in fleeting seconds,
Restless hearts begin to still.
Finding peace in soft reflections,
Murmurs heal with gentle will.

Fading echoes of the past,
Sway and swirl like autumn leaves.
In the quiet, truth illuminates,
Revealing paths we often grieve.

So let the whispers guide your way,
In the stillness, seek the light.
Murmured moments hold a magic,
Inviting souls to take flight.

Traces Left by Gentle Giants

In the forest, shadows linger,
Footprints faint, a tale unseen.
Trees that tower, wise and ancient,
Hold the secrets of the green.

Beneath their branches, stories woven,
Of time and seasons that once flowed.
Gentle giants, roots like whispers,
Breathe the life that they bestowed.

Nature's echoes, soft and solemn,
Speak of ages, strength untold.
In the rustling leaves, the wisdom,
Of those who walked the paths of old.

Every scar and every knot tells
Of wind and rain, of sunlit days.
In their presence, we find solace,
Guided by their steadfast ways.

Traces left by gentle giants,
Carved in earth, in memory's bloom.
Remind us of our fleeting journey,
As they shelter life in emerald room.

A Ponder in Nature's Arms

In stillness wrapped, the world awakens,
Nature cradles every sigh.
Mountains breathe, and rivers whisper,
A serenade beneath the sky.

Soft the petals drape like velvet,
Color spills from every seam.
In the meadow, thoughts unfurling,
Trade their worries for a dream.

Clouds drift by on gentle currents,
Mirror pools reflect the day.
In that pause, hearts find their rhythm,
Nature's arms, a warm array.

Every rustle, every heartbeat,
Echoes life in tranquil grace.
Amidst the chaos, find the stillness,
Hold the moment, embrace the space.

So linger here, with spirit open,
Trust the path that you will roam.
In nature's arms, a sweet surrender,
A timeless journey, a sacred home.

The Call of the Untold

In the twilight where dreams linger,
Voices beckon from afar.
Stories whispered in the silence,
Guided by a distant star.

Unseen paths await the daring,
Winds of change begin to stir.
With each step, the heart remembers,
Echoes lost in time's soft blur.

Mysteries like shadows beckon,
Dance upon the edge of night.
In the silence, secrets whispered,
Awake the soul to endless flight.

The call is rich, a song of wonder,
Filled with dreams yet to unfold.
In the stillness, hope is woven,
With threads of tales yet to be told.

So listen close, embrace the magic,
Let the stories take their hold.
For in the deep, the call is guiding,
To realms of dreams, forever bold.

Paths Uncharted in Solitude

In the woods where whispers roam,
Footsteps fade, I walk alone.
Moonlit beams through branches weave,
Guiding dreams that I conceive.

Silent paths beneath the pine,
Crickets sing, the stars align.
In the quiet, thoughts take flight,
Finding solace in the night.

The leaves will dance, the shadows play,
In solitude, I drift away.
Every turn, a story calls,
In the stillness, wonder enthralls.

Through the fog, the spirits murmur,
Unseen voices, soft and surer.
Heartbeat echoes, calm and clear,
In this refuge, I revere.

Paths untraveled, heartbeats swirl,
In the darkness, mysteries unfurl.
With every step, my soul ignites,
In solitude, I find the light.

Traces of Forgotten Dreams

In the attic of my mind,
Dusty whispers unwind.
Fragments of a time long past,
In shadows, memories are cast.

A lullaby of yesteryears,
Softly sighs and disappears.
Echoes linger, ghosts remain,
In the silence, there's the pain.

Old photographs, a faded hue,
Remind me of what once was true.
In the corners, stories hide,
Finding solace in what's denied.

With every dream, a promise made,
Yet, in time, the light will fade.
But in my heart, they always gleam,
These traces of forgotten dreams.

I hold them close, like cherished light,
Guiding me through endless night.
In their warmth, I find my way,
Through shadows, dawn will break the day.

The Stillness Between Heartbeats

In the quiet of a moment,
Time stands still, a soft lament.
Between each pulse, a world exists,
A gentle hush, a lover's kiss.

Whispers echo, silence reigns,
In the gaps, a heart sustains.
The breath between, a fragile thread,
Ties the living with the dead.

In the stillness, secrets dance,
Concealing pain, but offering chance.
Each heartbeat writes a tale anew,
In the pauses, love breaks through.

Moments linger, softly glow,
Building bridges, letting go.
In the space where silence lies,
Awakens dreams beneath the skies.

The rhythm flows, a sacred beat,
In the stillness, I find my seat.
With every pause, the world transforms,
In the stillness, life performs.

Hiding Amongst the Untraveled

In the wilds where few have gone,
Secrets linger in the dawn.
Footprints lost in tangled vines,
Nature whispers, life entwines.

Among the trees, I find my place,
Hidden from the world's embrace.
In the shadows, mysteries blend,
A quiet heart begins to mend.

The rustle of leaves, a calming sigh,
In solitude, I learn to fly.
In the hush, I breathe anew,
Amongst the paths, my spirit grew.

Nature's hymn, a gentle guide,
In its arms, I choose to hide.
Every breath, a step untold,
Adventure waits, both bold and cold.

Hiding deep where few may see,
In the untraveled, I am free.
With each heartbeat, I embrace,
The wild moments, my sacred space.

The Calm Between the Notes

In silence, whispers gently play,
Melodies linger, drift away.
Each pause a moment, deep and wise,
The heartbeats echo, softly rise.

A breath between the words we share,
Suspended dreams float in the air.
Gentle echoes mark the space,
Where time slows down, and fears erase.

In every chord, a story breathes,
A symphony of hopes and leaves.
The calm between the notes we find,
Is where the soul can unwind.

As music wraps around the night,
Soft shadows dance, a pure delight.
In rhythms lost, in beats that flow,
We find the strength to let love grow.

So listen well to every pause,
Embrace the silence with applause.
For in the calm, we understand,
The beauty lies in soft command.

Footprints of a Dreamer

Across the sands of time we tread,
With visions bright, and hopes widespread.
Each step we take, a tale untold,
In footprints deep, our dreams unfold.

Awake beneath the starry skies,
The universe within our eyes.
With every path that we explore,
New worlds await at destiny's door.

Beneath the moon's soft silver light,
We chase the dawn, we seek the bright.
With hearts alight and spirits free,
In every shadow, dreams agree.

Through valleys deep and mountains high,
We paint our futures, learn to fly.
In every journey, hand in hand,
Dreamers walk upon this land.

So let your spirit weave the night,
In every dream, find love and light.
In footprints left, we weave our fate,
With courage bold, we create great.

The Unfurling of Soft Horizons

As dawn awakens, colors blend,
The horizon stretched, a gentle friend.
With every hue, a promise glows,
In nature's arms, serenity flows.

The softest whispers of the breeze,
Invite the heart to find its ease.
A canvas wide, in gold and blue,
A quiet heart can start anew.

The mountains stand, in silence grand,
Guardians of dreams across the land.
In every sunrise, a story sings,
Of hope reborn and all it brings.

Through valleys rich, where shadows play,
The light of morning holds the sway.
With every moment, life refines,
In the unfurling of soft designs.

So breathe in deep, embrace the view,
In every dawn, find life anew.
The horizon whispers tales untold,
In colors bright, a life unfolds.

A Whisper in the Wilderness

In forests deep, where shadows play,
A whisper calls the lost to stay.
Beneath the trees, a secret shared,
In nature's heart, we find we're bared.

The rustling leaves, the babbling brook,
A symphony in every nook.
With every step on mossy ground,
A deeper peace is finally found.

In twilight's glow, the world transforms,
As colors fade, a stillness warms.
In every rustle, life emerges,
In tranquil streams, the spirit surges.

With every heartbeat, nature sings,
A chorus born from simple things.
In wild embrace, we come alive,
In whispers soft, our souls contrive.

So wander forth, let echoes lead,
In wilderness, plant every seed.
For in the quiet, truth exists,
A whisper's call, it can't be missed.

Footfalls on Forgotten Roads

Footfalls echo, soft and low,
Among the paths where wildflowers grow.
Shadows linger, tales untold,
Memories wrapped in the folds of gold.

Whispers of ancients, sighs of the past,
Through tangled branches, shadows cast.
Every step, a story unfolds,
In the heart where the silence holds.

Faded footprints in the dust,
Nature's canvas, laid in trust.
Time stands still, a gentle guide,
On forgotten roads where spirits abide.

Paths diverge, yet they lead home,
In the heart, no need to roam.
With every footfall, secrets spill,
On forgotten roads, we find our will.

In the twilight's soft embrace,
We lose ourselves in a timeless space.
Footfalls fade as night descends,
But the journey lives, where the road bends.

The Calm Before Discovery

Beneath the veil of softening light,
The world holds its breath in fading twilight.
Each moment hangs, so steeped in grace,
A hush envelops this sacred space.

Stars begin to peek through the haze,
Illuminating dreams of brighter days.
The silence whispers secrets deep,
Of wonders waiting, of promises to keep.

Laden with hope, the heart beats slow,
As shadows dance and breezes flow.
In this calm, frustration fades,
With every heartbeat, a new path is laid.

The air is thick with potential's call,
Every sigh treasured, no fear of fall.
In quiet valleys, visions stir,
Ready to blossom as passions blur.

Here, we linger; fear drifts away,
Embracing change as night turns to day.
The calm before the waves of delight,
Where dreams awaken and take flight.

Muffled Murmurs in the Meadow

In the meadow, secrets are spun,
Beneath the gaze of the setting sun.
Muffled murmurs of grass and breeze,
Nature's whispers, soft as the leaves.

Crickets chirp, their rhythm plays,
In harmony with the end of days.
A lullaby sung by the world so bright,
As shadows stretch and blend with night.

Wildflowers sway in the twilight's glow,
Each petal a tale, each stem a flow.
The hymn of nature fills the air,
In every breath, a timeless prayer.

Through the stillness, dreams take flight,
In the cradle of fading light.
Muffled murmurs weave and blend,
In the meadow's heart, where time transcends.

The night unfolds, the stars will gleam,
The meadow whispers, a tender dream.
In the silence, our souls align,
Together in wonder, forever we shine.

Wanderer's Embrace of Tranquility

In the wanderer's heart lies a gentle peace,
A refuge found where the storms will cease.
Footsteps trace the paths of old,
Under skies of azure, stories unfold.

Each step whispers of lands unknown,
In the echoes of worlds where dreams have flown.
With open arms, the horizon calls,
In tranquil embrace, the wanderer sprawls.

Mountains loom, majestic and vast,
While valleys cradle the shadows cast.
Nature's beauty, a sacred song,
In the wanderer's soul, where they belong.

Streams of silver, forests alive,
In tranquility, the spirit thrives.
Lost in the moment, so free to roam,
Every journey crafted, every path a home.

Beneath the stars, a promise made,
In the wanderer's heart, fears will fade.
Embracing tranquility, lose all strife,
In the vastness, find the essence of life.

www.ingramcontent.com/pod-product-compliance
Ingram Content Group UK Ltd.
Pitfield, Milton Keynes, MK11 3LW, UK
UKHW021939200125
4187UKWH00037B/739

9 781805 616023